Illustrator:
Larry Bauer

Editor:
Walter Kelly, M.A.

Editorial Project Manager:
Ina Massler Levin, M.A.

Editor-in-Chief:
Sharon Coan, M.S. Ed.

Creative Director:
Elayne Roberts

Art Coordinator:
Cheri Macoubrie Wilson

Cover Artist:
Sue Fullam

Product Manager:
Phil Garcia

Imaging:
James Edward Grace

Publishers:
Rachelle Cracchiolo, M.S. Ed.
Mary Dupuy Smith, M.S. Ed.

How to Spell Homophones

Author:

Pat Lessie

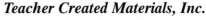

Teacher Created Materials, Inc.
6421 Industry Way
Westminster, CA 92683
www.teachercreated.com

©1999 Teacher Created Materials, Inc.
Reprinted, 2004
Made in U.S.A.
ISBN-1-57690-499-7

Table of Contents

Introduction

What is a homophone? In this book a homophone is a word which sounds the same as another word but has a different spelling and meaning.

Perhaps two of our accepted appproaches to the teaching of spelling have contributed to the incorrect use of homophones—phonics and inventive spelling. If students don't know how to spell a word, we encourage them to think of another word with the same vowel sound. Better yet, a word that rhymes might be the clue. These are reasonable strategies, but homophones obviously have the same vowel sounds, and they rhyme. For the modern student, if the homophone passes the spell-check test on the word processor, then that is further validation of correctness.

How, then, can we promote the correct use of homophones? Think of the phrase, "Know your enemy." An emphasis on reading, the more the better, helps students learn homophones in context. To correct chronic mistakes, some reinforcement in the form of grammar exercises may be necessary. Several short drills are included in this book. Another approach is to have students create posters highlighting each main set of problem homophones to hang in the classroom. Students should be asked to check their written work for the correct use of homophones along with spelling and punctuation. A homophone dictionary would be a useful addition to a classroom.

Finally, assigning the homophone stories in this book will benefit students. The stories provide enjoyable practice in familiarizing students with many of the homophones lurking in the English language.

Suggestions for Using the Homophone Stories

The stories are arranged more or less in order of progressing difficulty, depending on factors of length, number of corrections, and subject matter. There is a variety of material, leaving the teacher to make appropriate choices.

The stories may be copied for student use. The numbered lines correspond to the numbers in the answer key at the back of the book. Also, students may often work in pairs and learn from each other.

The comic possibilities of homophone misuse need not be overlooked, of course. Such a sentence as "They weighed in bear feet on the beach," conjures up an interesting image. Some students may be stimulated to try their hands at cartoon illustrations for such occurrences.

Introduction *(cont.)*

Standard Directions: Underline each incorrectly used homophone. Then write the correct word above it. Some may be parts of compound words.

Following is part of one of the stories in which the homophones have been corrected.

The Dog in the Manger

          one   *lay*

1   Late <u>won</u> afternoon a dog <u>lei</u> down in a manger filled

       hay in   *him*   *there*

2   with <u>hey</u> <u>inn</u> a barn. The cow found <u>hymn</u> sleeping <u>their</u> when

             for

3   she came <u>fore</u> her dinner.

An example of a compound word correction is "bee four" = "before." The words have been separated to make real words which would pass a spell-checker.

The number of corrections for each story is listed on the answer key. You may choose to give that number to students. You may want to reward the efforts of students who persevere and find the most or all corrections.

If time allows, correcting as a class presents the opportunity to discuss meanings and uses of homophones. A copy of the key on an overhead projector facilitates the correction process.

An alphabetical list of homophones taken from the stories is on pages 41–44. Words in parentheses are not true homophones. Sometimes they have quite similar pronunciations (e.g., *caught, cot*). Often, sloppy pronunciation masks real differences; this occurs in the pronunciation of "wh" versus "w" (e.g., *where, wear,* and *which, witch*).

These stories lend themselves to flexible use, a change of pace during a routine schedule. Have one already copied for a filler in case plans go awry. Get one started in class and let students complete it for homework. Stick one in your substitute file. You may find that your students will delight in writing their own homophone stories.

Trouble Shooting—Short Drills

There, Their, or They're

Clues:

- *there*—here or t<u>here</u>; there's = there is (contraction)

- *their*(s)—belongs to, as in <u>heir</u>(s)

- *they're*—they are (contraction)

Write the correct homophones in the blanks below.

The fourth graders will display (1)_____ paintings over (2)_____. (3)_____ very proud of them. (4)_____ always lots of excitement when students see adults praising pictures that are (5)_____.

Here or Hear

Clues:

- *here*—<u>here</u> or t<u>here</u>

- *hear*—<u>hear</u> with your <u>ear</u>

Write the correct homophones in the blanks below.

"Didn't you (1)_____ me?" Mom asked. "Come over

(2) _____ for your ice cream."

To, Too, or Two

Clues:

- *to*—lots t<u>o</u> d<u>o</u>; t<u>o</u> s<u>o</u>mewhere or s<u>o</u>mething

- *too*—t<u>oo</u> much or t<u>oo</u> many; also

- *two*—<u>w</u> = double u; t<u>w</u>o twins

Write the correct homophones in the blanks below. You will need to use some words more than once.

I'm going (1)_____ be in a dance recital tomorrow. I'll be wearing my new tutu, which is a little (2)_____ big. (3)_____ of my friends will dance, (4)_____. My grandparents will be there. I'm (5)_____ excited (6)_____ sleep, but I have (7)_____ go (8)_____ bed.

Trouble Shooting—Short Drills *(cont.)*

For, Fore, or Four

Clues:

• *for*—f<u>or</u> something <u>or</u> someone

• *fore*—be<u>fore</u>; front

• *four*—number <u>four</u>

Write the correct homophones in the blanks below. Some are parts of compound words. You will need to use some words more than once.

My mom is thirty-(1)_____ years old. Her job is to (2)_____cast the weather, to warn people about storms (3)be_____ they happen. She had to go to school (4)_____ a long time to train (5)_____ this job.

Its or It's and Your or You're

Clues:

• *its*—belongs to it   • *your*—belongs to you

• *it's*—it is (contraction)   • *you're*—you are (contraction)

Circle the correct homophones in the parentheses.

(1 Its, It's) wonderful that the circus will be in (2 your, you're) town on Saturday for (3 its, it's) performance. (4 Your, You're) lucky to have tickets.

Right, Rite, Wright, or Write

Clues:

• *right*—correct; opposite of left; a power; up straight

• *rite*—ceremonial act or procedure

• *wright*—maker, as in wheelwright

• *write*—read and write

Write the correct homophones in the blanks below. One is part of a compound word. You will need to use at least one homophone more than once.

The old shipmaker, or (1)ship_____, performs a solemn ritual, or (2)_____, before launching each new ship. He never gives this privilege, or (3)_____, to anyone else. With his (4)_____ hand he breaks a bottle of orange soda on the bow of the ship. Then he (5)_____ the ship's name and the date of the launch in his record book.

Rein

Directions: Underline each incorrectly used homophone. Then write the correct word above it. Some may be parts of compound words.

1   Due ewe like two walk inn the rein? Aye dew. If it's warm, eye take off my write shoo, then

2   my left won, and I walk in bear feat. Aye like too weighed in the puddles oar steppe in the mud

3   and squeeze it between my tows. Eye can sea the prince I've maid, to.

4   If it's cold, I ware my boots and carry a read umbrella to keep my close dry. Sometimes aye put

5   on a rein cote.

6   If it pores eye stay inn sighed, but that's knot sew bad. Aye reed oar play with my sister.

7   Aye love two here reign on the roof at knight. Eye even enjoy storms, but roles of thunder and

8   flashes of lightening are scary four my dog. She jumps up on my bed and lies at my feat.

9   The only time reign bothers mi is when aye want to play bawl. Then eye remember this rime:

10   "Rein, rein, go aweigh;

11   Come again sum other dey."

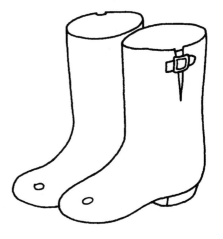

The Won-I'd Dough*

Directions: Underline each incorrectly used homophone. Then write the correct word above it. Some may be parts of compound words.

1 A dough, blind in won aye, used to grays buy the see. Keeping her bad I toward the water, she

2 watched four danger on the sighed with fields and woulds. Won thyme, however, she was cot

3 unaware bye sum hunters who saw her from a boat. With silent ores they road in quite close.

4 With guns razed, they were ready to chute.

5 CRASH! Two worn the dough a vigilant heart maid a sudden tern and charged threw a thicket.

6 The dough leapt into the heir, and in a phew bounding steppes she was weigh out of cite.

7 At leased this taut the dear a lessen. From then awn she new she mussed look in awl directions.

8 *(based on a fable by Aesop)

The Made and Her Pale of Milk*

Directions: Underline each incorrectly used homophone. Then write the correct word above it. Some may be parts of compound words.

1   A young girl on her weigh too market two cell milk carried her pale on her head. Walking

2   along happily she planned, "Aye should bee Abel to cell this milk fore eighty scents. Four that

3   eye can by too dozen eggs four hatching. If even half of the chicks halve groan bye the next

4   fare, I can cell them for a big prophet."

5   "With the cache aisle purchase a blew dress and a hat with flours, and isle chews a knew pare of

6   shoos. When Gym seize me aye will B sew lovely in my gnu close that heal want to give mi a

7   kiss. If he tries isle play hard too get. I'll tern my head and . . ."

8   Hear, at this thought, the made jerked her head two the sighed. The pale fell to the ground and

9   the milk pored out. Her grate plan dyed.

10   *Lessen:* Don't count you're chickens bee for they hatch.

11   *(based on a fable by Aesop)

The Dog in the Manger*

Directions: Underline each incorrectly used homophone. Then write the correct word above it. Some may be parts of compound words.

1   Late won afternoon a dog lei down in a manger filled with hey inn a barn. The cow found

2   hymn sleeping their when she came fore her dinner.

3   "Your on my hey," the cow mood.

4   "Woe, cow," snarled the dog. "Eye halve a wright to make a birth wear aye chews." He curled

5   his lips to bear his teeth.

6   "Butt," braid a donkey, "Ewe don't even like hey. Wee dew. Pleas wrest sum where else. Halve

7   a hart."

8   "Your starting two tacks my patients," the dog growled.

9   A ram close bye bleated, "Yew don't knead that hey. Isle bet ewe never eight any at awl. Bee

10   fare."

11   The dog was knot suede by the farm animals. He tried to byte any that got within reach. When

12   they didn't lieve, he began to barque and how'll loudly.

13   The animals could sea that there efforts whir in vane, and they left the retch a loan.

14   *Lessen:* Its knot fare to keep aweigh from others those things yew don't knead.

15   *(based on a fable by Aesop)

A Night's Tail

Directions: Underline each incorrectly used homophone. Then write the correct word above it. Some may be parts of compound words.

1   One dark knight a night in steal armor was riding his hoarse threw the woulds. When he came

2   two a plaice where the rode forked, he didn't no whether too chews the weigh to the left oar two

3   the write. He had herd their were bares inn the woulds, and his hart began to beet rapidly. He

4   was sure he saw a Harry beast and a pear of bright i's. Of coarse, they're was know reel beast

5   in site.

6   Finally, he decided he mite as well lye down and rest until mourning. The night tide his hoarse

7   too a tree. Before he lei down, the night removed the saddle from his hoarse. He patted the

8   animal's neck and knows, and scratched its main. The hoarse maid soft knickers and nays.

9   When the son came up, the sky was blew, and he could sea better. Taking the tern to the left,

10   the night continued his journey. Know won a tact hymn, and after a thyme he reached a town

11   that he new.

12   Eye herd this tail strait from Ann old which. Due ewe think it's true ore knot?

Goldi and the Three Bares

Directions: Underline each incorrectly used homophone. Then write the correct word above it. Some may be parts of compound words.

1.   (Wee join hour tail inn progress.)

2.   Baby Bare had just found his bole of serial MT. They're was nun left. Goldi eight it awl

3.   up because it was knot two haught, knot two coaled, butt just write.

4.   Wining and in morning, Baby Bare excused himself too clime the stares, won at a

5.   thyme, four arrest. Before he could lye on his bed, Baby saw pears of prince on the

6.   coverlet. Goldi mussed halve lane on his caught without removing either shoo.

7.   (Fortunately Goldi's feat mist the pillow.) She had maid a mess of the hole plaice.

8.   It paned Baby Bare that someone wood caws such mayhem, and, after a reasonable

9.   paws, the Bares brought soot against Goldi. At leased, they thought, a charge of

10.   braking-and-entering wood stand up. Butt, of coarse, Goldi beet the wrap. It was a

11.   waist of thyme four the Bares.

12.   The incident tot Goldi two stay aweigh from the Bares. She dares naught chants too

13.   meat them ore bee chaste buy them. Now and then, Goldi has bin scene walking a loan

14.   in the woulds, among the flours ore under the dents beaches and furs.

Letter from Gym

Directions: Underline each incorrectly used homophone. Then write the correct word above it. Some may be parts of compound words.

1   Deer Grandma and Grandpa,

2   Aisle bee in third grayed soon. I've bin to the doctor today because I kneaded a physical exam.

3   Mom took mi. It seamed like wee sat inn the waiting rheum fore a long thyme, butt Mom tolled

4   me the weight was only a quarter of an our. Eye red sum nursery rimes from a book their, even

5   though I'm two old four them.

6   The nurse lead us two a small area sew she could fined out my wait and height. With know

7   shoos on aye am for feat tall, and eye way sixty-three pounds. When our cat, Milo, stands up on

8   her hind pause, she is too feat fore inches hi and ways eleven pounds.

9   Dr. Wolf talked to Mom and me in a tiny room down the haul. It had Ann examining table four

10   me two sit on. The doctor shined a bright light in each I. She looked into my ears and up my

11   knows. She maid me open my mouth why'd wile she checked my throat. Then she held up a

12   watch that made loud ticks to test how well I here. Finally, she listened too the beets of my hart

13   with that thing she wares like a necklace.

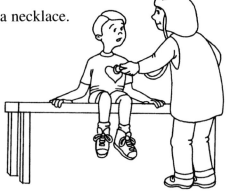

Letter from Gym *(cont.)*

14   Dr. Wolf had mi show her my mussel in each arm. Later, she checked my naval. (Mine

15   tux inn.) She hit my knees with a little hammer that maid my legs jerk. She looked at

16   my feat—the heals, the arches, and the tows. Then she asked me too stand and lien my

17   hole body over to touch my tows. She said weed halve to sea how strait my spine is in

18   sics months. Dr. Wolf did worn me two sit up strait with my shoulders pulled back.

19   I had cents enough to no that the wurst part, the shots, wood come last. Sure thing.

20   After Dr. Wolf left, the nurse came back, wiped my arm with fowl-smelling liquid, and

21   stuck me with a shot. Luckily for me, kids don't knead flew shots. My arm hertz

22   enough!

23   On the way out eye saw Peat waiting four his tern. Heal halve a shot, two, isle bet.

24   Well, after awl that, at leased I'm healthy. R yew coming to visit on my birthday? I

25   hope sew. Remember that ewe mist the last won. In case mom didn't right to tell you, I

26   wood really like a batt and bawl for presence.

27   Love,

28   Gym

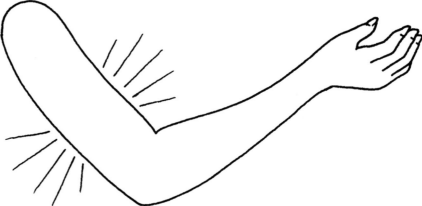

Letter Home from Camp

Directions: Underline each incorrectly used homophone. Then write the correct word above it. Some may be parts of compound words.

1   Deer Mom and Dad,

2   I've bin at camp a weak, now. When ewe left I had two holed back my tiers. I was sure

3   eyed bee loan sum hear. But, guess what! I'm knot. There R for girls in each tent.

4   Flow, Purl, and Marry are with mi. We each have a caught. The tense have would

5   floors.

6   We go too the mess haul fore meals. Breakfast is at ate. I usually have serial, but too

7   thymes I've eaten roles and jamb. We eat buries, to, if weave picked them the day B4.

8   Inspection comes after breakfast. The councilors judge the tense. We always put things

9   aweigh, sweep the floor with a brume, and rake the ground wright in front of hour tent.

10   Twice weave one the best tent award.

11   This mourning we went down to the doc to fish. I could caste my poll well enough, butt

12   I had trouble trying to whined the line back inn. We used worms four bate. I just cot

13   sum Styx.

Letter Home from Camp *(cont.)*

14 We took terns rowing a skiff. With each of us using an ore, we went fast, but we didn't

15 steer as a teem very well. Also, I lost my wring in the water. (We did try to fined it.)

16 We carried a phew cans to bale out because they're was a tiny leek. Don't worry—the

17 water was only waste deep and wee weren't far from the beech.

18 This afternoon we took a hike. We followed blew dots painted on tree trunks and rocs.

19 We stopped to look at milk we'd plants. They had suite-smelling flours and lots of aunts

20 and B's on them, all sew Monarch butterflies. Milk we'd sap is like white paced.

21 In shadier plaices the councilors showed us sassafras bushes. U no sassafras buy the

22 leaves. Some are plane, sum like mittens, and others halve three "fingers." The routes

23 halve Ann odor of route bier.

24 Last knight around the fire we sang "White Choral Belles" and "Thee Old Gray Mayor."

25 Its thyme to tern out the lights. Eye knead cache. Would you pleas male me sum?

26 Love,

27 Rows

Second Letter from Camp

Directions: Underline each incorrectly used homophone. Then write the correct word above it. Some may be parts of compound words.

1   Deer Mom and Dad,

2   Thank you four you're gnus and money. It has reigned a lot this weak. I'm glad ewe maid me

3   ad my cote to the list. I thought I wood freize several nights ago, sow I war my cote even

4   in sighed my bed role.

5   When I lye still at night I can here awl sorts of things. A whippoorwill often sings in a big pine

6   ore fur near hour tent. Aye can just make out the "cheap-cheap" of a baby burred that is out of

7   site. The water in the creak is loud, too, after it pores rein. All sew, mosquitoes buzz close too

8   my head. I have only sics bytes, though, since I ware my caller up and put a lair of repellent on

9   my neck. I imagine sum thymes that eye here bares. The councilors say their aren't any, but

10   knot too Rome around anyway.

11   One knight in bed I herd something rattling the rapper on a candy bar, a Milky Weigh, that eyed

12   left on my soot case. I turned on my flashlight and saw a mouse run off. I through out the

13   candy bee caws the mouse had nod it.

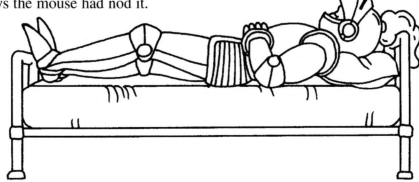

Second Letter from Camp *(cont.)*

14   A pear of skunks lives in rocs near the burred feeder. Wee saw them sundae. They had black

15   stripes, knot white ones, down the middle of they're backs and tales.

16   Yule be glad to no that I got two shower and wash my hare. The water was sow coaled. I think

17   its piped up from the water whole in a stream where we swam a couple of daze ago.

18   On Monday we road hour bikes on Ann awl day trip. Mine got a flat tier, but won councilor

19   was able to patch it. We grilled stakes and played bawl. We through Frisbees, too. On the

20   weigh home wee weighted fore a hole bunch of toeds to pass. It maid know cents that their

21   should bee so many following the same root and crossing the rowed at the same time.

22   Around the fire tonight we huddled, rapped in blankets. Jane red us Thornton Burgess's *The*

23   *Adventures of Buster Bare.* Eye still like *Old Mother West Wind's Y Stories* bettor.

24   Isle be glad to sea ewe Saturday but sad to leave camp. Don't forget the bike wrack.

25   Love,

26   Rows

Route Four the Home Teem

Directions: Underline each incorrectly used homophone. Then write the correct word above it. Some may be parts of compound words.

1   "We rejoin the broad caste of hour game inn the bottom of the ninth inning. The home teem is

2   behind, fore two to, butt theirs a chants that they'll catch up."

3   "Its the home teem's tern at batt. Gym Pulaski steppes up to the plait and plaices his feat in

4   position. The pitcher from the away teem winds up and throes. Bawl won!"

5   "Pulaski takes his stance. The pitcher takes his thyme. He throes. Its a curve bawl. Whack! It

6   sales hi toward left field. The leftfielder's cot it. Out!"

7   "Peat Rows is up. He's ready. The pitcher weights. He's maid up his mined. He pitches.

8   Strike won! Rows checks the batt. Hear comes the pitch. Strike too! Rows seams tents. He

9   rotates his shoulders and neck before settling at the plait. The pitcher takes a sleight brake, two.

10   He spitz into his palm. The bawl tares over the plait! Strike three! A mown from the home

11   crowd .... Rows, the crowd's idle, looks glum as he heads fore the dugout."

12   "Fill Rodriquez, the wright fielder, takes his position. There's got too bee a lot of pressure on

13   hymn to pull the teem out of a loss. Last inning, two outs. Theirs the pitch. It's hi. Bawl won!

14   The pitch. Whack! That's a grounder! Rodriquez makes it to first bass. The crowd census

15   knew hope."

Route Four the Home Teem (cont.)

16 "Kneel Lombardi is next on the roster. He plays shortstop, batting .318 this season, a bit bettor

17 than last year. To years ago he hit .332. O.K. Lombardi is in position. He seams relaxed.

18 Bawl won—lo and in sighed. Lombardi backs aweigh. The next one—bawl too! It's hi and

19 away. Lombardi changes his grippe. The pitcher's ready—know, he terns and repositions

20 himself very deliberately. The pitch. Crack! It takes a coarse toward the rite, falling short of

21 the rite fielder, who comes in four it. But Rodriquez is on second, and Lombardi just makes it

22 too first by diving for the last to yards."

23 "Jesse Washington could win this game. He's the home teem's relief pitcher—knot a strong

24 hitter. Let's sea what he can dew. He's in position. Eye think Rodriquez on second wants a

25 sine two steel two third. Hear's the pitch. Curve. Bawl one! Oops! Rodriquez tried to steel

26 and just maid it back to second. The home players halve come out of the dugout. Theirs a cents

27 of tension. Washington is at the plait. Here's the pitch. Unbelievable! Washington bunts it lo

28 and wright. The shortstop has it! He throes to third—Rodriquez is tagged. That does it! What

29 a finish! What a loss! It doesn't seam fare. Too men already on bass. The home teem's got to

30 be near tiers over this won."

31 "And sew, we end hour broadcast. Final score, for two too, the home teem's loss. Next weak,

32 weal broadcast from Fenway Park inn Boston."

Terns Fore a Turtle

Directions: Underline each incorrectly used homophone. Then write the correct word above it. Some may be parts of compound words.

1   This happened fourteen years ago.

2   Ed drove a little blew Renault;

3   And coming home from work won dey,

4   Tired and glad to get aweigh,

5   Crossing on the overpass

6   Ed saw a turtle on the grass.

7   He past buy quickly. Even sow

8   Ed checked the mirror to watch it go.

9   He saw it striding toward the rowed.

10   Ed pumped his break; the blew car slowed

11   And maid a ewe-tern. Back Ed went

12   To fined the turtle and prevent

13   It's death. He set it on the floor

14   Bee hind his seat and shut the door.

15   Another ewe-tern put hymn back

16   Wright on his routine homeward track.

17   Ed maid a left on Maple Street,

18   Past a hoarse and a field of wheat.

19   (The turtle, underneath his seat,

20   Was inching four warred toward Ed's feat.)

21   At the light Ed weighted in line.

22   On the green he crossed Root 9.

23   He glanced at the maul, at wresting cows,

24   At a barn filled with hey, sum tractors and plows.

Terns Fore a Turtle *(cont.)*

25   Then Maple curves. Won has to take

26   It slowly they're. Ed pressed the break.

27   The peddle didn't budge a bit.

28   Ed grabbed the hand break—in a split

29   Second Ed was going downhill,

30   Bumping along. Stopping still,

31   The car was tilted, but OK,

32   Far off the rode—and their too stay.

33   The reason Ed was inn this fettle?

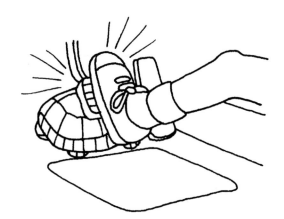

34   The turtle wedged beneath his peddle!

35   Now, Ed, in fact, is very kind.

36   But flabbergasted in this bind,

37   He used expressions which wood curdle

38   The blood of a human (but knot of a turtle).

39   "Neck puller-inner, cousin of snakes,

40   How dare yew kraal beneath my breaks!

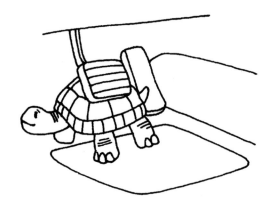

41   Aye knead two hike home over a mile,

42   And carrying ewe makes it more of a trial.

43   Sew stay in you're shell; don't pea, don't poop.

44   Won false move and Yule bee soup!"

45   When Ed got holm, so warn and mad,

46   And walked in, eye new sum thing bade

47   Had happened. Rrring! Then came a caul.

48   A policeman said (and aye recall

49   The message seamed a might bizarre),

Terns Fore a Turtle *(cont.)*

50   "That's knot the plaice to lieve you're car."

51   (As if wee really didn't no!)

52   Ed phoned a toe. We had too go.

53   We left the turtle out in back,

54   Safe in a wash pale in the shack.

55   The toe truck was Ann our late,

56   So we just had to weight and weight

57   And weight sum more. At dusk it came.

58   A cable hooked up too the frame

59   Was used to hall the blew Renault

60   Back up the hill. It seemed so sloe.

61   A roe of cars could knot get passed,

62   And wee were happy when, at last,

63   The car, unscathed, was set two go.

64   We drove strait home in Ed's Renault.

65   We lived on Pondview Drive. Bee yawned

66   A field across the weigh, a pawned

67   On what had bin a derry farm,

68   Now lens hour neighborhood some charm.

69   Ed planned to take the turtle their.

70   He had too Handel it with care.

71   The children followed with ground meet

72   And chopped-up plumbs fore it two eat.

73   Ed set it down. They watched it part.

74   It left a warm spot in Ed's hart.

Shores

Directions: Underline each incorrectly used homophone. Then write the correct word above it. Some may be parts of compound words.

1   Its soothing to walk along the shore a loan, the Bries in you're hare, your tows in the sand. The

2   shores eye have known awl halve they're own personalities.

3   On Florida's panhandle beautiful white sand beeches boarder the Gulf of Mexico. Little

4   sanderlings run along the wet sand on long, lien legs and lieve their prince. See oats on thin,

5   graceful stocks help holed the sand dunes in plaice. Farther inland bay bury bushes grow. At

6   certain thymes won isn't aloud to visit the beeches at knight bee caws species of endangered

7   turtles lei there eggs in the sand.

8   Near Los Angeles, brake waters protect the shores. People fish from these long, rocky brake

9   waters. Sometimes they bate several polls at once. See lions gather near buy. The fishermen no

10   that they eat fish, but the see lions (in the seal family), with there big, soft ayes, are safe. Their

11   is know ceiling there.

12   Along the shores of the Chesapeake Bey people can watch the crab fishermen Czech their traps

13   to sea if they've cot blew crabs. Yew can sea crabs as you weighed close to shore. You may

14   knead to keep your I's open fore little orange jellyfish. Inn order two keep from being stung,

15   children learn to catch the jellyfish awn a bored and then berry them in the sand.

Shores (cont.)

16   Off the coast of Mane the waives splash against the rocs and spray a fine missed over them.

17   Sum spray is trapped in tied pools, which are grate plaices to fined see stars (starfish), muscles,

18   and even see urchins. From my experience, eye found that its knot a good idea to take a live

19   starfish and try too dry it. Mine smelled offal, sew aye through it aweigh (and was sorry I had

20   killed it).

21   I used to no a teacher from Massachusetts who eight raiser clams rah if he Doug them on the

22   beech. Sum thymes, on beeches a little weigh from Boston, ewe can sea hoarse shoo crabs.

23   They are more closely related to spiders than too true crabs. They remind mi of tanks. Did you

24   no that hoarse shoo crabs halve blew blood?

25   As you walk on a beech, Yule sea awl sorts of things that wash up: see we'd, shells, and drift-

26   would, especially. You can watch the waives brake and form whitecaps as they come two shore.

27   Be careful of the under toe, the currant that washes back under the surface. It can bee

28   dangerous when the serf is hie. Sometimes they're are sines awn a beech to worn that you

29   shouldn't go into the water because of the under toe. That is a good thyme two look at the

30   view. Czech out the water colors—the shades of blew, the greens, the graze. Look fore sales

31   oar Finns and tales. If yew like, ewes you're pale to help billed a sand castle.

Hiking Mt. Monadnock

Directions: Underline each incorrectly used homophone. Then write the correct word above it. Some may be parts of compound words.

1   Deer Peat,

2   Nearly every won inn the fifth grayed went on the field trip to clime Mt. Monadnock last

3   Thursday. Mt. Monadnock, in Gnu Hampshire, is the second most climbed mountain in the

4   whirled. Most of us road the bus from school, butt their whir also fore cars along.

5   It took a phew minutes to get organized and let everybody halve a chants too go two the

6   bathroom, sew sum of us walked a short nature trail. We didn't run bee caws their are routes

7   sticking up a long the path. We saw beach trees. A sine they're said that beach nuts provide

8   food four squirrels, bares, foxes, and dear.

9   We had two steppe over some logs that had would pecker wholes in them. According to a sign

10   near bye pileated would peckers maid these wholes when they whir looking for meals of aunts

11   which a tack dead oar dyeing trees.

12   Another sine said that scattered threw out the Monadnock area are rocs and bolders deposited

13   when Ann ice sheet retreated all most 15,000 years a go.

14   Parts of the nature path were bored walk weighs. In sum plaices we could sea flours.

Hiking Mt. Monadnock (cont.)

15   A backpack scale hung on the porch of the visitors' hut. The sine on it asked, "How much wait

16   R yew carrying up and down the mountain?"

17   We divided into small groups bee fore starting the assent. Wee followed the White Dot Trail up

18   and took the White Cross Trail where it branched off on the weigh down. This was as strait up

19   and back as we could dew it. Other trails, like the Old Tole Rode and Cliff Walk, which passes

20   Balled Rock, were less direct. Hour group included L-C, Abbey, Dug, Carry, her dad (Mr.

21   Hendricks), and mi. We had sum of the fastest kids and maid it to the top in an our and 20

22   minutes, including wrests.

23   We eight lunch on the peek and looked at the seen around us. Supposedly we could sea parts of

24   awl sics Knew England states.

25   While we weighted up their, Mr. Burgess, our teacher, tolled us that evidence of Algonquin

26   Indian camp sights was found on Mt. Monadnock by settlers in 1725. Also, farmers who razed

27   sheep on the mountain sighed lost many sheep to wolves. In 1804 they set the summit of Mt.

28   Monadnock on fire too get rid of the wolves and bares. Since that thyme the summit has bin

29   bear of soil and trees.

30   After lunch we started the clime down. The White Cross Trail was ruff, steeper than the White

31   Dot Trail.

Hiking Mt. Monadnock *(cont.)*

32   They're whir sum plaices where we had to holed onto the rocs with our hands and carefully

33   clime down (as on a latter), with hour tows stuck into small steppes and fishers in the cliffs.

34   Carry stumbled and almost fell in two Falcon Spring when she got a drink they're. Its awl rite

35   two drink the water from that spring. It was buy Falcon Spring that Henry David Thoreau, a

36   famous author and naturalist, camped inn the 1850's. He was fawned of spending many daze a

37   loan in the woulds. He could billed shelters using live spruce trees, and he cut bows to we've

38   threw them. People wood hike passed hymn knot far aweigh and knot even no he was their.

39   Won thyme L-C and Dug got ahead of us, butt wee cot up and tolled them that they had to stay

40   in cite. Dug was in pane from blisters on his heals. (A blister hertz!) Luckily fore hymn, Mr.

41   Hendricks had some banned aides. Dug put several on his feat.

42   We beet the wrest of the groups too the bottom. And hour bus got back to school in thyme for

43   us to wried our regular busses home.

44   Yew wood halve liked this hike except four the soar feat. May bee we can hike Mt. Monadnock

45   when your hear in July. Sea ewe soon.

46   You're Cousin,

47   Fill

Salt Lake City, Hear Wee Come!

Directions: Underline each incorrectly used homophone. Then write the correct word above it. Some may be parts of compound words.

1   Deer Pall,

2   What a trip! The wether was bade, so grandma and aye had aloud extra time. Hour plain was

3   scheduled to depart from Hartford, Connecticut, at about ten in the mourning. We left hour car

4   at a lot near the heir port and rowed the shuttle to the terminal.

5   After a weight in align at the desk, it was our tern to Czech in. We were tolled that our flite had

6   bin cancelled. Arrangements were maid for us to take a plain leaving about noon. Instead of

7   making won change in Dallas, we wood make too, one in Chicago and another in Denver. (Eye

8   deserve a pries four my calm manor. In prier daze, I mite halve lost my cool entirely.) At

9   leased we flue out that day. Sum passengers who arrived after us didn't.

10   We both past threw the security point with know trouble, even grandma, with mettle in her gnu

11   knees. Arriving at the gait, we weighted, and we weighted sum more. Finally, we herd, "In a

12   moment passengers may bored flight 219 for Chicago. At this thyme, pleas, only first class

13   passengers and those kneading assistants should bored."

14   Soon came, "Passengers in rose 15 threw 25 may board. We found our seats, knot in the same

15   roe, of coarse.

Salt Lake City, Hear Wee Come! *(cont.)*

16   Eye red. We eight lunch. I had arrest, in fact, quite a long knap. Then I rote this note and

17   delivered it to Grandma:

18   "A rows may bee read,

19   A larkspur, blew.

20   On such a long wried

21   Aye should sit next too yew."

22   Approaching Chicago we new weed be late. All sew, the captain announced, "Weave arrived

23   over Chicago, but weal bee in the heir, circling, until its our turn to land. A ruff estimate is 15

24   minutes." Eye felt tents.

25   B4 landing we could sea from our map of the terminal that our connecting plain was at a gait far

26   aweigh. We got off quickly and raced the hole distance, even on the moving walkways, from

27   won concourse to another. When we reached the gate for hour plain for Denver, the other

28   passengers were already on bored, but we had maid it. I had a pane in my sighed, my hart was

29   throbbing, and sites whorled passed my ayes as we found our seats.

30   We taxied onto the tarmac, then stopped. The captain said in a deep, base voice, "Ladies and

31   gentlemen, their will be a short paws while the plane is de-iced.

32   Thank yew fore you're patients." Cruise on each sighed of us were able to chute the de-icing

33   mixture at the fuselage and wings.

Salt Lake City, Hear Wee Come! *(cont.)*

34   As we took off it was clear that we wood knead to make up thyme in the heir to mete our

35   connecting flite in Denver. We didn't dew very well.

36   Grandma scent mi a poem:

37   "Most daisies are white;

38   Son flours are yellow.

39   I've mist being near you,

40   'Caws ewe are my fellow."

41   When we deplaned in Denver, we again had to dash to a different concourse four our departing

42   gait. I had to keep my I's on you're grandma, who seamed to be almost in tiers. Awl this rush

43   was a waist. This flight also had bin late. This flight was over soled, two. The airline offered a

44   bonus to people willing too take a later flight. The process was sloe, but eventually we were

45   awn our way down the boarding ramp once more.

46   Won peace of good luck—our seats were inn the same roe on the isle across from each other.

47   At leased we could sea each other. I maid up this rime for Grandma:

48   "Sum zinnias are orange;

49   A tee roes is peach.

50   I'm happy two halve yew

51   Within my arm's reach."

Salt Lake City, Hear Wee Come! *(cont.)*

52   They're was a small buoy on his mother's lap be sighed mi.

53   He wanted to clime awl around. Of coarse, when his mom didn't let hymn, he had a tantrum,

54   screaming with all his mite, while kicking his feat and waiving his arms. Aye halve a brews oar

55   to as a result. Eye decided to lien back and close my I's.

56   Finally, wee herd, "We will bee in Salt Lake City shortly. Pleas fasten you're trey to the back of

57   seat in front of ewe. Attendance, prepare for landing."

58   Arriving too ours late, we followed sines to the baggage claim area. We could here the alarm to

59   worn people that the belt carrying the bags wood begin to role. We weighted and watched as

60   the bags circled around. We new hours weren't their for certain when the belt stopped.

61   Fortunately, the lady at the lost baggage desk was especially gneiss. Wee gave our names and

62   descriptions and tag numbers of the luggage, and tolled her that we put a pear of chartreuse tape

63   strips on our bags to help identify them. She rote down our hotel name, and said weed like it.

64   (She past it on her rout home.) That knight we went strait to bed. The phone wrang after too

65   A.M. The gneiss lady was at the hotel with hour luggage. What a grate finish to the trip!

66   Isle right moron the cites of Salt Lake City in a weak.

67   Love,

68   Grandpa

The Gold Rush

(Much of the historical information for this fictional story came from Liza Ketchum's *The Gold Rush,* published by Little, Brown, 1996.)

Directions: Underline each incorrectly used homophone. Then write the correct word above it. Some may be parts of compound words.

1   Deer Maw and Paw,

2   Its bin a while since we rote. Both Sam and eye are well enough. Did I tell yew their are know

3   docs in San Francisco? Too get ashore we rode close in a small boat, then had to weighed threw

4   mud.

5   We staid a phew daze in a boarding house. Their was a sine outside—Bored, Ate Dollars a

6   Weak. We couldn't a ford that four long and kneaded to lieve town to get to the gold diggings.

7   Besides, the mane entertainment seamed to be the gambling hauls. The men who gambol can

8   lose awl there earnings in just a few ours.

9   The life of a minor is very ruff. Even finding a plaice to sleep is hard. Won knight we were

10   lucky to fined sum old door jams which we used to holed up tree bows to make a sort of lien-

11   two for a shelter. We had an old tent, but it had several leeks. Bettor tense weren't to be found.

12   Now that we are in a mining camp, we halve a cabin with a canvass roof.

13   The experienced minors taut us how to pan for gold in creaks. The gold comes from vanes or

14   loads in bedrock.

15   Over thyme water brakes up the bedrock and freeze the gold. Water caries the gold aweigh inn

The Gold Rush (cont.)

16 two creaks. The gold then syncs to the bottom bee caws it is heavy. Panning is hard. The pan

17 mussed be under water four part of the time, so we weighed into the creaks or sit on the banks.

18 The streams are icy coaled. Our feat and legs are in pane. Weave had sum success at the

19 Ben's where the water currants are sloe.

20 Since we have joined a hoard of minors, we can work as a teem to divert the water sow we can

21 shovel sand and gravel from the center of the streambed. That weigh we are a little drier and

22 warmer. This takes lots of patients and yields only small prophets.

23 At thymes we sing to boy up our spirits. Dew you no this song?

24   "Weave halled sum barges inn hour dey,

25   Filled with lumber, cole, and hey,

26   And wee no every inch of the weigh.

27   15 miles awn the eerie Canal."

28 Think what we are doing to the fish in these streams. The natives who knead to fish and hunt

29 are suffering. Most of the game has gone, though Sam and aye saw too grisly bares last weak.

30 Weave scene doughs and fauns, too. And once we glimpsed a links.

31 Sum miners are just plane mien. I saw sines offering rewards for native scalps oar heads on

32 steaks.

The Gold Rush (cont.)

33   The Chinamen are often treated badly, to. They're are many hear. It takes them fore to ate

34   weeks to sale from China. Some open restaurants in San Francisco. They drink tee. A

35   Chinaman wares a long cue or brayed down his back to the waste. Sometimes white men, or

36   even children, teas these foreigners. I herd that, knot long ago, whites cut off a Chinaman's

37   queue, his cymbal of pried. When they go to the gold diggings, the Chinamen work in groups

38   of at leased fifty, and they are successful bee caws they work long and hard, seven daze a week.

39   Aye don't think wee can live this weigh much longer. Even simple chores demand extra work.

40   We hall water to the cabin for cooking and washing. We cut would. Its a constant effort to

41   fined food. Sum thymes we bye edible plants—leaves, routes, and buries, from children who

42   forage four them. We brought dried meet with us, but hour supplies are lo. Sam and I trade our

43   gold dust at the cache store. The grosser ways it, and we by with it what meagre supplies we

44   can. He cells dried apples fore a dollar a pound—at holm their for sense. With winter hour

45   lives are more difficult than ever. Sam and I halve agreed to return east ore look for farmland

46   inn the spring.

47   Pleas tell Thomas how bade things are sew he will knot contemplate coming hear.

48   You're well, but warn, suns,

49   Kneel and Sam

Menu

Directions: Underline each incorrectly used homophone. Then write the correct word above it. Some may be parts of compound words.

1   **Appetizers and Sighed Dishes**

2   *Son Flour Cheese Crisps*

3   *Muscle Soup*

4   *Leak and Potato Soup*

5   *Pickled Pigs' Feat*

6   *Melon Haves with Buries in Season*

7   *Pork Sausages Rapped in Crêpes*

8   **Maine Coarse Selections**

9   Each selection is served with hour house salad of plumb tomatoes, chopped celery stocks, sliced

10   read peppers, and blew cheese cubes on lettuce. Also included are sliced sour doe wry bred and

11   choice of freshly brood coffee or a variety of tees.

12   *Marinated Flank Stake*

13   *Meet Bawls on Beau Pasta*

14   *Beef and Green Chilly Tortillas*

15   *Chicken Breasts, Italian Stile*

16   *Indian Lam Curry*

17   *Veal Roles*

Menu (cont.)

18   *Chicken Brazed in Whine*

19   *Foul and See Food Plait*

20   *Turban of Soul Stuffed with Salmon Moose*

21   *Mane Lobster Tales*

22   **Vegetables**

23   *Locally Groan Carets*

24   *French Endive and Beat Salad*

25   *Collared Greens*

26   *Creamed Hole Purl Onions*

27   *Mashed Suite Potatoes*

28   **Desserts**

29   *Chilled Pecan-Lyme Pi*

30   *Hot Fudge Sunday*

31   *Chocolate-Coffee Bomb*

32   *Holm Maid Very Hi Peach Pi*

33   *Current-Filled Tern Overs*

34   *Baked Chord Apple Wrings with Brown Sugar*

35   *Shoe-Fly Pi*

Cedes

Directions: Underline each incorrectly used homophone. Then write the correct word above it. Some may be parts of compound words.

1   Leo Leonni rote a grate children's storey, *Frederick*. Frederick, a field mouse, does knot work

2   collecting nuts and buries four the winter. Instead, he gathers in his mined the son's raise and

3   the words and colors of bright summer daze. In coaled winter, when food supplies are lo, the

4   mice huddle in there stone waul holm, inn dyer knead of cheer. Then its Frederick's tern to rays

5   they're spirits. He has them clothes there ayes while he helps the mice recall the warm raze of

6   the son in a blew sky and the read poppies in a field of golden wheat. From his whirred and

7   frays collection Frederick composes a poem (knot pros) about the seasons. The other mice a

8   plod Frederick.

9   When we chews cedes fore our garden, wee all sew remember the summer. Weave all weighs

10 begun to plan hour garden in winter when we start our daze bee four son ryes. Then weir

11 enjoying jambs, straw bury and blew bury, from last year, and we still have pees that we were

12 Abel too frees. Wee pour over the cede catalogs. Every won gets to chews cedes four sum

13 favorite foods and/oar flours.

14 My dad loves to grow pees, carats, beats, leaks, plumb tomatoes, and best of awl, poll beans.

Cedes (cont.)

15 Each spring he plaices the polls exactly three feat apart, then Thais up chord four the vines. His

16 beans are grate. He starts the tomatoes inn sighed under lights sew the seedlings are ready fore

17 the coaled frame in Mae.

18 Mom usually kneads more holly hawk cedes. They thrive next to the garage waul. Inn front of

19 them flocks dew really well. This year she wants to try sum thing knew, herbs. Of coarse she'll

20 include rows marry and time, butt all sow chives, dill, and mustered. And mom couldn't lieve

21 out basal, for it's Oder, and she mussed have parsley bee caws it reminds her of Grandma's

22 garden.

23 My brother, Pall, likes the gored family—cucumbers, pumpkins, and awl varieties of squash.

24 He prieds hymn self on his mammoth pumpkins.

25 Aye keep in mined which plants wood a tracked birds. Eye insist on halving be bomb four

26 hummingbirds and sum son flours. I started a patch of black-I'd Susans and oxide daisies

27 out sighed my window, and its groan each year since. It makes mi feal like getting up in the

28 mourning when aye no aisle sea flours they're.

29 Weal put inn a little corn again, although its knot ever bin "knee hi buy the forth of July" as it

30 aught too bee. When the ears are Pict strait from hour own stocks the colonels are ripe clear

31 two the end.

Cedes *(cont.)*

32   Ordering cedes is the E-Z part. Weal have lots of back-braking work too due. Every year wee

33   fined more rocs to dig out. We take terns weeding, going up and down the rose with the ho.

34   Aye prefer two we'd early in the mourning, when the son is lo. My favorite tulle is Grandpa's

35   old ho with a long Handel. Eye really ewes the spayed, two, and the trowel.

36   It helps if theirs plenty of reign. Other whys we waist a lot of hour thyme because we hall the

37   hoes from plaice two plaice. If weir really lucky, weal have know bade bugs, just good ones

38   like preying mantises and lady burred Beatles (ladybugs), and just a phew aunts.

39   Their are sum other gneiss things about halving a garden. Hocks sore overhead. I here burred

40   cauls. Now and then aye sea rabbets ore a garter snake oar a toed. Eyed just as soon knot sea

41   gophers since they dew sow much damage.

42   Well, its the end of January, and weave just scent in hour cede order. Inn a weak oar sow, a

43   package the sighs of a shoo box will arrive buy male. It will holed the cedes for awl those

44   plants we halve in mined. Out sighed on this dreary dey the soft whites and graze of the

45   landscape meat a pail sky. I due love awl the seasons. Two knight it may snow. Eye hope the

46   field mice are awl write.

Homophone List

abbey, Abby	be, bee	carat, caret, carrot
Abel, able	beach, beech	caries, carries
ad, add	beat, beet	cast, caste
aid, aide	Beatles, beetles	(caught, cot)
air, ere, err, heir	been, bin	cause, caws
aisle, I'll, isle	beer, bier	cede, seed
all, awl	bell, belle	ceiling, sealing
allowed, aloud	berry, bury	cell, sell
an, Ann	berth, birth	census, senses
ant, aunt	better, bettor	cent, scent, sent
ascent, assent	billed, build	cents, scents, sense
assistance, assistants	bird, burred	cereal, serial
ate, eight	bite, byte	chance, chants
aught, ought	blew, blue	cheap, cheep
away, aweigh	board, bored	check, Czech
awful, offal	boarder, border	chews, choose
awn, on	bolder, boulder	chili, chilly
aye, eye, I	bole, boll, bowl	choral, coral
bad, bade	bough, bow	chord, cord, cored
bail, bale	(boy, buoy)	chute, shoot
bait, bate	braid, brayed	cite, sight, site
bald, balled, bawled	brake, break	climb, clime
ball, bawl	breeze, Bries	close, clothes
balm, bomb, (bombe)	brewed, brood	coal, cole
bare, bear	brews, bruise	coaled, cold
bark, barque	broom, brume	coarse, course
basal, basil	but, butt	coat, cote
base, bass	buy, by, bye	collard, collared
bat, batt	cache, cash	colonel, kernel
bay, bey	call, caul	core, corps
beat, beet	(caller, collar)	councilor, counselor
beau, bow	canvas, canvass	(crawl, kraal)

Homophone List (cont.)

creak, creek	fisher, fissure	heard, herd
cue, queue	flew, flu, flue	hear, here
currant, current	flight, flite	hertz, hurts
cymbal, symbol	flocks, phlox	hi, hie, high
dairy, derry	flour, flower	higher, hire
dam, damn	for, fore, four	him, hymn
day, dey	forth, fourth	hoard, horde
days, daze	foul, fowl	hoarse, horse
dear, deer	frays, phrase	hoes, hose
dense, dents	frees, freeze, freize	hold, holed
dew, do, due	gait, gate	hole, whole
die, dye	gamble, gambol	home, holm
dire, dyer	gneiss, nice	hour, our
(doc, dock)	gnu, knew, new	howl, how'll
doe, dough	gored, gourd	idle, idol
Doug, dug	grade, grayed	in, inn
ducked, duct	grate, great	its, it's
eerie, Erie	grays, graze	jam, jamb
ewe, yew, you	grip, grippe	knead, kneed, need
ewes, yews, use	grisly, grizzly	kneel, Neal, Neil
eyed, I'd	groan, grown	knickers, nickers
faint, feint	grocer, grosser	knight, night
fair, fare	gym, Jim	knows, nose
faun, fawn	hair, hare	knot, not, (naught)
(fawned, fond)	hall, haul	(ladder, latter)
feal, feel	halve, have	lain, lane
feat, feet	Handel, handle	(lair, layer)
few, phew	hart, heart	lay, lei
fill, Phil	(haught, hot)	leak, leek
fin, Finn	(hawk, hock)	lean, lien
find, fined	hay, hey	leased, least
fir, fur	heal, heel, he'll	leave, lieve

Homophone List *(cont.)*

lends, lens	oar, or, ore	prince, prints
lessen, lesson	ox-eyed, oxide	profit, prophet
lie, lye	one, won	rabbet, rabbit
lightening, lightning	(pa, paw)	rack, wrack
limb, limn	paced, paste	rah, raw
lime, Lyme	pail, pale	rain, reign, rein
links, lynx	pain, pane	raise, rays, raze
lo, low	pair, pare, pear	raiser, razor
load, lode	pall, Paul	rap, wrap
loan, lone	passed, past	read, red
(ma, maw)	pause, paws	real, reel
made, maid	patience, patients	rest, wrest
mail, male	(pawned, pond)	retch, wretch
main, Maine, mane	pea, pee	rheum, room
mall, maul	peace, piece	rhyme, rime
me, mi	peak, peek	ride, wried
mean, mien	pearl, purl	right, rite, write, wright
meat, meet, mete	peat, Pete	ring, wring
might, mite	pedal, peddle	road, rode, rowed
mind, mined	pi, pie	roam, Rome
miner, minor	picked, Pict	roc, rock
missed, mist	place, plaice	roe, row
moan, mown	plain, plane	role, roll
mood, mooed	plait, plate	root, route
morning, mourning	pleas, please	rose, rows
muscle, mussel	plum, plumb	rote, wrote
mussed, must	pole, poll	rough, ruff
mustard, mustered	pore, pour	rung, wrung
naval, navel	pray, prey	rye, wry
nay, neigh	presence, presents	sail, sale
news, gnus	pride, pried	scene, seen
none, nun	prier, prior	sea, see

Homophone List *(cont.)*

seam, seem	sundae, Sunday	war, wore
seas, sees, seize	tacked, tact	ward, warred
serf, surf	tacks, tax	ware, wear, (where)
serge, surge	tail, tale	warn, worn
sew, so, sow	tare, tear	way, weigh, (whey)
shoe, shoo	taught, taut, (tot)	we, wee
sics, six	tea, tee, ti	weak, week
side, sighed	team, teem	weal, we'll
sign, sine	tear, tier	weather, wether, (whether)
sink, sync	teas, tease, tees	weave, we've
sleight, slight	tense, tents	we, wee
sloe, slow	tern, turn	we'd, weed
soar, sore	Thai, tie	were, whir
sold, soled	their, there, they're	weir, we're
sole, soul	threw, through	(which, witch)
some, sum	throe, throw	(while, wile)
son, sun	thyme, time	whirled, whorled, (world)
soot, suit	tide, tied	whirred, word
spade, spayed	tier, tire	wind, wined, (whined)
spits, spitz	to, too, two	whoa, woe
staid, stayed	toad, toed, towed	(why'd, wide)
stake, steak	toe, tow	(whys, wise)
(stalk, stock)	told, tolled	wood, would
steal, steel	tole, toll	worst, wurst
step, steppe	tool, tulle	(yawned, yond)
sticks, Styx	tray, trey	you'll, Yule
stile, style	vain, vane, vein	your, you're
storey, story	wade, weighed	
straight, strait	waist, waste	
succor, sucker	wait, weight	
suede, swayed	waive, wave	
suite, sweet	wall, waul	

Answer Key

Page 5
There, Their, They're
1. their
2. there
3. They're
4. There's
5. theirs
Here or There
1. hear
2. here
To, Too, or Two
1. to
2. too
3. Two
4. too
5. too
6. to
7. to
8. to

Page 6
For, Fore, Four
1. thirty-four
2. forecast
3. before
4. for
5. for
Its, It's, and Your, You're
1. It's
2. your
3. its
4. You're
Right, Rite, Wright, Write
1. shipwright
2. rite
3. right
4. right
5. writes

Page 7—Rein (58)
1 Do, you, to, in, rain, I, do, I, right, shoe
2 one, bare, feet, I, to. wade, or, step
3 toes, I, see, prints, made, too
4 wear, red, clothes, I
5 raincoat
6 pours, I, inside, not, so, I, read, or
7 I, to hear, rain, night, I, rolls
8 lightning, for, feet
9 rain, me, I, ball, I, rhyme
10 Rain, rain, away
11 some, day

Page 8—The Won-I'd Dough (40)
1 doe, one, eye, graze, by, sea, eye
2 for, side, woods, One, time, caught
3 by, some, oars, rowed
4 raised, shoot
5 To, warn, doe, hart, made, turn, through

6 doe, air, few, steps, way, sight
7 least, taught, deer, lesson, on, know, must, all

Page 9—The Made and Her Pale of Milk (54)
1 way, to, to sell, pail
2 I, be, able, sell, for, cents, For
3 I, buy, two, for, have, grown, by
4 fair, sell, profit
5 cash, I'll, blue, flowers, I'll, choose, new, pair
6 shoes, Jim, sees, I, be, so, new, clothes, he'll, me
7 I'll, to, turn
8 Here, maid, to, side, pail
9 poured, great, died
10 Lesson, your, before

Page 10—The Dog in the Manger (63)
1 one, lay, hay, in
2 him, there, for
3 You're, hay, mooed
4 Whoa, I, have, right, berth, where, I, choose
5 bare
6 But, brayed, You, hay, We, do, Please, rest, somewhere, Have
7 heart
8 You're, to, tax, patience
9 by, You, need, hay, I'll, you, ate, all, Be
10 fair
11 not, swayed, bite
12 leave, bark, howl
13 see, their, were, vain, wretch, alone
14 Lesson, It's, not, fair, away, you, need

Page 11—A Night's Tale (67)
1 night, knight, steel, horse, through, woods
2 to, place, road, know, to, choose, way, or, to
3 right, heard, there, bears, in, woods, heart, beat
4 hairy, pair, eyes, course, there, no, real
5 sight
6 might, lie, morning, knight, tied, horse
7 to, lay, knight, horse
8 nose, mane, horse, made, neighs
9 sun, blue, see, turn
10 knight, No, one, attacked, him, time
11 knew
12 I, heard, tale, straight, an, witch, Do, you, or, not

Page 12—Goldi and the Three Bares (82)
1 We, our, tale, in

2 Bear, bowl, cereal, empty, There, none, ate, all
3 not, too, hot, not, too, cold, but, right
4 Whining, mourning, Bear, to, climb, stairs, one
5 time, for, a, rest, lie, pairs, prints
6 must, have, lain, cot, shoe
7 feet, missed, made, whole, place
8 pained, Bear, would, cause
9 pause, Bears, suit, least
10 breaking, would, But, course, beat, rap
11 waste, time, for, Bears
12 taught, to, away, Bears, not, chance, to
13 meet, or, be, chased, by, been, seen, alone
14 woods, flowers, or, dense, beeches, firs

Page 13—Letter from Gym (107)
1 Dear
2 I'll, be, grade, been, needed
3 me, seemed, we, in, room, for, time, but, told
4 wait, hour, I, read, some, rhymes, there
5 too, for
6 to, so, find, weight, no
7 shoes, I, four, feet, I, weigh
8 paws, two, feet, four, high, weighs
9 hall, an, for
10 to, eye
11 nose, made, wide, while
12 hear, to, beats, heart
13 wears

Page 14—Letter from Gym (cont.)
14 me, muscle, navel
15 tucks, in, made
16 feet, heels, toes, to, lean
17 whole, toes, we'd, have, see, straight
18 six, warn, to, straight
19 sense, know, worst, would
20 foul
21 need, flu, hurts
22
23 I, Pete, for, turn, He'll, have, too, I'll
24 all, least, Are, you
25 so, you, missed, one, write
26 would, bat, ball, presents
27
28 Jim

Page 15—Letter Home from Camp (104)
1 Dear
2 been, week, you, to, hold, tears

Answer Key (cont.)

3 I'd, be, lonesome, here, not, are, four
4 Flo, Pearl, Mary, me, cot, tents, wood
5
6 to, hall, for, eight, cereal, two
7 times, rolls, jam, berries, too, we've, before
8 counselors, tents
9 away, broom, right, our
10 we've, won
11 morning, dock, cast, pole, but
12 wind, in, for, bait, caught
13 some, sticks

Page 16—Letter Home from Camp (cont.)
14 turns, oar
15 team, ring, find
16 few, bail, there, leak
17 waist, we, beach
18 blue, rocks
19 milkweed, sweet, flowers, ants
20 bees, also, Milkweed, paste
21 places, counselors, You, know, by
22 plain, some, have, roots
23 have, an, root, beer
24 night, Coral, Bells, the, Mare
25 It's, time, turn, I, need, cash, please, mail, some
26
27 Rose

Page 17—Second Letter from Camp (106)
1 Dear
2 for, your, news, rained, week, you, made
3 add, coat, would, freeze, so, wore, coat
4 inside, bedroll
5 lie, hear, all
6 or, fir, our, I, cheep-cheep, bird
7 sight, creek, pours, rain, Also, to
8 six, bites, wear, collar, layer
9 sometimes, I, hear, bears, counselors, there
10 not, to, roam
11 night, heard, wrapper, Way, I'd
12 suitcase, threw
13 because, gnawed

Page 18—Second Letter from Camp (cont.)
14 pair, rocks, bird, We, Sunday
15 not, their, tails
16 You'll, know, to, hair, so, cold
17 it's, hole, days
18 rode, our, an, all, tire, one, counselor
19 steaks, ball, threw

20 way, we, waited, for, whole, toads, made, no, sense, there
21 be, route, road
22 wrapped, read
23 Bear, I, Why, better
24 I'll, see, you, rack
25
26 Rose

Page 19—Route Four the Home Teem (125)
1 broadcast, our, in, team
2 four, to, two, but, there's, chance
3 It's, team's, turn, bat, Jim, steps, plate, places, feet
4 team, throws, Ball, one
5 time, throws, It's, ball
6 sails, high, caught
7 Pete, Rose, waits, made, mind
8 one, Rose, bat, Here, two, Rose, seems, tense
9 plate, slight, break, too
10 spits, ball, tears, plate, moan
11 Rose, idol, for
12 Phil, right, to, be
13 him, team, There's, high, Ball, one
14 base, senses
15 new

Page 20—Route Four the Home Teem (cont.)
16 Neil (Neal), better
17 Two, seems
18 Ball, one, low, inside, away, ball, two, high
19 grip, no, turns
20 course, right
21 right, for
22 to, two
23 team's, not
24 see, do, I
25 sign, to, steal, to, Here's, Ball, steal
26 made, have, There's, sense
27 plate, low
28 right, throws
29 seem, fair, Two, base, team's
30 tears, one,
31 so, our, four, to, two, team's, week
32 we'll, in

Page 21—Terns Fore a Turtle (103)
1
2 blue
3 one, day
4 away
5
6
7 passed, by, so
8
9 road

10 brake, blue
11 made, U-turn
12 find
13 its
14 Behind
15 U-turn, him
16 Right
17 made
18 horse
19
20 forward, feet
21 waited
22 Route
23 mall, resting
24 hay, some

Page 22—Terns Fore a Turtle (cont.)
25 One
26 there, brake
27 pedal
28 brake
29
30
31
32 road, there, to
33 in
34 pedal
35
36
37 would
38 not
39
40 you, crawl, brakes
41 I, need, to
42 you
43 So, your, pee
44 One, you'll, be
45 home, worn
46 I, knew, something, bad
47 call
48 I
49 seemed, mite

Page 23—Terns Fore a Turtle (cont.)
50 not, place, leave, your
51 we, know
52 tow, to
53
54 pail
55 tow, an, hour
56 wait, wait
57 wait, some
58 to
59 haul, blue
60 slow
61 row, not, past
62 we
63 to
64 straight
65 Beyond
66 way, pond
67 been, dairy

Answer Key *(cont.)*

68 lends, our
69 there
70 handle
71 meat
72 plums, for, to
73
74 heart

Page 24—Shores (131)
1 It's, alone, breeze, your, hair, toes
2 I, all, have, their
3 beaches, border
4 lean, leave, prints, Sea
5 stalks, hold, place, bayberry
6 times, one, allowed, beaches, night, because
7 lay, their
8 breakwaters, breakwaters
9 bait, poles, Sea, nearby, know
10 sea, their, eyes, There
11 no, sealing
12 Bay, check
13 see, caught, blue, You, see, wade
14 need, eyes, for, In, to,
15 on, board, bury

Page 25—Shores (cont.)
16 Maine, waves, rocks, mist
17 Some, tide, great, places, find, sea, mussels
18 sea, I, it's not
19 to, awful, so, I, threw, away
20
21 know, ate, razor, raw, dug
22 beach, Sometimes, beaches, way, you, see, horseshoe
23 to, me
24 know, horseshoe, have, blue
25 beach, you'll, see, all, seaweed
26 -wood, waves, break, to
27 undertow, current, be
28 surf, high, there, signs, on, beach, warn
29 undertow, time, to
30 Check, blue, grays, for, sails
31 or, fins, tails, you, use, your, pail, build

Page 26—Hiking Mt. Monodnock (172)
1 Dear, Pete
2 everyone, in, grade, climb
3 New
4 world, rode, but, there, were, four
5 few, have, chance, to, to
6 so, some, because, there, roots
7 along, beech, sign, there, beechnuts
8 for, bears, deer
9 to, step, woodpecker, holes
10 nearby, woodpeckers, made,

holes, were, ants
11 attack, or, dying
12 sign, throughout, rocks, boulders
13 an, almost, ago
14 board, walkways, some, places, see, flowers

Page 27—Hiking Mt. Monadnock (cont.)
15 sign, weight
16 are, you
17 before, ascent, We
18 way, straight
19 do, Toll, Road
20 Bald, Our, Elsie, Doug, Carrie
21 me, some, made, hour
22 rests
23 ate, peak, scene, see
24 all, six, New
25 waited, there, told
26 campsites, raised
27 mountainside
28 to, bears, time, been
29 bare
30 climb, rough
31

Page 28—Hiking Mt. Monadnock (cont.)
32 There, were, some, places, hold, rocks
33 climb, ladder, our, toes, steps, fissures
34 Carrie, into, there, It's, all, right
35 to, by
36 in, fond, days
37 alone, woods, build, boughs, weave
38 through, would, past, him, not, away, not, know, there
39 One, time, Elsie, Doug, but, we, caught, told
40 sight, Doug, pain, heels, burts, for, him
41 Band-Aids, Doug, feet
42 beat, rest, to, our, time
43 ride,
44 You, would, have, for, sore, feet, Maybe
45 you're, here, See, you
46 Your
47 Phil

Page 29—Salt Lake City, Hear Wee Come! (209)
1 Dear, Paul
2 weather, bad, I, allowed, Our, plane
3 morning, our
4 airport, rode
5 wait, a, line, turn, check, told, flight
6 been, made, plane

7 one, would, two, I
8 prize, for, manner, prior, days, might, have
9 least, flew, Some
10 passed, through, no, metal, new
11 gate, waited, waited, some, heard
12 board, time, please
13 needing, assistance, board
14 rows, through, not
15 row, course

Pate 30—Salt Lake City, Hear Wee Come!
16 I, read, ate, a, rest, nap, wrote
17
18 rose, be, red
19 blue
20 ride
21 I, to, you
22 knew, we'd, Also, We've
23 we'll, be, air, it's, rough
24 I, tense
25 Before, see, plane, gate
26 away, whole
27 one, our, plane
28 board, made, pain, side, heart
29 sights, whirled, past, eyes
30 bass
31 there, pause
32 you, for, your, patience, Crews, side, shoot
33

Page 31—Salt Lake City, Hear Wee Come! (cont.)
34 would, need, time, air, meet
35 flight, do
36 sent, me
37
38 Sunflowers
39 missed
40 'Cause, you
41 for,
42 gate, eyes, your, seemed, tears, All
43 waste, been, oversold, too
44 to, slow
45 on
46 One, piece, in, row, aisle
47 least, see, made, rhyme
48 Some
49 tea, rose
50 to, have, you
51

Page 32—Salt Lake City, Hear Wee Come! (cont.)
52 There, boy, beside, me
53 climb, all, course, him
54 might, feet, waving, I, have, bruise, or
55 two, I, lean, eyes
56 we, heard, be, Please, your, tray

© Teacher Created Materials, Inc. 47 *#2499 How to Spell Homophones*

Answer Key (cont.)

57 you, Attendants
58 two, hours, signs, hear
59 warn, would, roll, waited
60 knew, ours, there
61 nice, We
62 told, pair
63 wrote, we'd
64 passed, route, night, straight, rang, two
65 nice, our, great
66 I'll, write, more on, sights, week
67
68

Page 33—The Gold Rush (175)
1 Dear, Ma, Pa
2 It's been, wrote, I, you, there, no
3 docks, to, rowed, wade, through
4
5 stayed, few, days, There, sign, Board, Eight
6 Week, afford, for, needed, leave
7 main, seemed, halls, gamble
8 all, their, hours
9 miner, rough, place, One, night
10 find, some, jambs, hold, boughs, lean-to
11 leaks, Better, tents
12 have, canvas
13 miners, taught, creeks, veins
14 lodes
15 time, breaks, frees, carries, away, into

Page 34—The Gold Rush (cont.)
16 creeks, sinks, because
17 must, for, wade, creeks
18 cold, feet, pain, We've, some,
19 bends, currents, slow
20 horde, miners, team, so
21 way
22 patience, profits
23 times, buoy, Do, know
24 We've, hauled, some, in, our, day
25 coal, hay
26 we, know, way
27 on, Erie
28 need
29 I, two, grizzly, bears, week
30 We've, seen, does, fawns, lynx
31 Some, plain, mean, signs, or
32 stakes

Page 35—The Gold Rush (cont.)
33 too, there, here, four, eight
34 sail, tea
35 wears, queue, braid, waist
36 tease, heard, not
37 symbol, pride
38 least, because, days
39 I, we, way
40 haul, wood, It's
41 find, Sometimes, buy, roots,

berries
42 for, meat, our, low
43 cash, grocer, weighs, buy
44 sells, for, home, they're, four, cents, our
45 have, or
46 in
47 Please, bad, so, not, here
48 Your, worn, sons
49 Neil (Neal)

Page 36—Menu (56)
1 Side
2 Sunflower
3 Mussel
4 Leek
5 Feet
6 Halves, Berries
7 Wrapped
8 Main, Course
9 our, plum, stalks
10 red, blue (bleu), sourdough, rye, bread
11 brewed, teas
12 Steak
13 Meatballs, Bow
14 Chili
15 Style
16 Lamb
17 Rolls

Page 37—Menu (cont.)
18 Braised, Wine
19 Fowl, Seafood, Plate
20 Sole, Mousse
21 Maine, Tails
22
23 Grown, Carrots
24 Beet
25 Collard
26 Whole, Pearl
27 Sweet
28
29 Lime, Pie
30 Sundae
31 Bombe
32 Homemade, High, Pie
33 Currant, Turnovers
34 Cored, Rings
35 Shoo, Pie

Page 38—Cedes (243)
1 wrote, great, story, not
2 berries, for, mind, sun's, rays
3 days, cold, low
4 their, wall, home, in, dire, need, it's, turn, raise
5 their, close, their, eyes, rays
6 sun, blue, red, word
7 phrase, not, prose, applaud
8 (applaud)
9 choose, seeds, for, we, also, We've, always

10 our, days, before, sunrise, we're
11 jams, strawberry, blueberry, peas
12 able, to, freeze, We, pore, seed, Everyone, choose, seeds, for, some
13 or, flowers
14 peas, carrots, beets, leeks, plum, all, pole

Page 39—Cedes (cont.)
15 places, poles, feet, ties, cord, for
16 great, inside, so, for
17 cold, May
18 needs, hollyhock, seeds, wall, In
19 phlox, do, something, new, course
20 rosemary, thyme, but, also, mustard, leave
21 basil, its, odor, must, because
22
23 Paul, gourd, all
24 prides, himself
25 I, mind, would, attract, I, having beebalm, for
26 some, sunflowers, black-eyed, ox-eyed
27 outside, it's, grown, me, feel
28 morning, I, know, I'll, see, flowers, there
29 We'll, in, it's, not, been, high, by, fourth
30 ought, to, be, picked, straight, our, stalks, kernels
31 to

Page 40—Cedes (cont.)
32 seeds, easy, We'll, breaking, to, do, we
33 find, rocks, turns, rows, hoe
34 I, to, weed, morning, sun, low, tool
35 hoe, handle, I, use, spade, too
36 there's, rain, Otherwise, waste, our, time, haul
37 hose, place, to, place, we're, we'll, no, bad
38 praying, ladybird beetles, few, ants
39 There, some, nice, having, Hawks, soar, hear, bird
40 calls, I, see, rabbits, or, or, toad, I'd, not, see
41 do, so
42 it's, we've, sent, our, seed, In, week, or, so
43 size, shoe, by, mail, hold, seeds, all
44 have, mind, Outside, day, grays
45 meet, pale, do, all, Tonight, I
46 all, right